The Supply of the Spirit

Warren Hunter

Sword Ministries International
Branson, Missouri

The Supply of the Spirit
Published by:
Sword Ministries International
3044 Shepherd of the Hills
Exprwy Ste 649
Branson, MO 65616
ISBN 1-889816-23-X

Cover design & book production by:
DB & Associates Design Group, Inc.
dba Double Blessing Productions
P.O. Box 52756, Tulsa, OK 74152
www.dbassoc.org

Printed in the United States of America.

Contents

Preface

At first, I thought that writing this book would be easy, but as I worked on this book, I found myself stepping deeper and deeper into God's unbound, unlimited ocean. The vastness of the supply of the Spirit grows more and more as you meditate upon this revelation and flow of the Holy Spirit. What we're about to undertake and explain has been in the workings for several years. Originally this book was supposed to be the first book that I was going to write, but the Holy Spirit had me take it up occasionally over several years.

I also do not want to reiterate on the subject unlimited anointing as I share on this subject in *Volume 2 of The Unlimited Realm.* However, some of the thoughts on unlimited anointing are required in this book to bring across a more comprehensive aspect concerning the supply of the Spirit.

I pray that as you read this book it will bring you into a greater dimension of the flow of the power of God in you, through you, and about you. May God's great grace abound toward you so that you may become sons and daughters of God releasing the greater works that you have been destined to flow in according to the power of the Holy Spirit.

Introduction

Perhaps some of my favorite childhood memories were those of going swimming at the beach in Durban, South Africa. Enjoying the sights and sounds of the ocean was a thrilling experience. From the beach, the rolling waves looked very intimidating. It was always quite a challenge to swim past them. Many times the waves peaked well over six feet, causing most people to remain on the shore or just play around in the shallow water. What they did not realize, was that past all the thundering waves was calmer seas. Our life in God is very similar to this scenario. In Ezekiel 47, the author tells us to move from ankle deep waters until we are swimming in the abounding ocean of His supply.

Because our time on earth is limited, there is an urgency in the realm of the spirit to access the supply of the Spirit. Using the layout of the tabernacle as an example, we must go past the brazen alter, past the bronze laver, and past the veil. We must enter into the Holy of Holies where the Ark of the Covenant is and into the *Most* Holy Place where God's presence abides. In order to accomplish this spiritual journey, we must go *deeper* than we have ever gone before in our relationship with God, beyond the shallow waters and past the thundering waves, until we flow into the ocean of Almighty God.

Deep calls unto deep at the noise of Your waterfalls; all your waves and billows have gone over me.

Psalm 42:7

How do we enter into a deeper more intimate relationship with God?

How do we exceed a shallow, superficial existence and access this bountiful ocean of God's supply?

How can we allow the supply of the Spirit to flow through us continually?

Many Christians are desperately seeking answers to these questions today. The purpose of this book is to answer them and relay the principles that were crucial in my own life to going further with God than I ever had before. However, no principle or text can accomplish anything without an intimate and focused *prayer life*. Christians must come to the realization that everything we achieve is through the limitless power of *God's grace* and divine favor toward us, His children. When we combine the truths of His word with these forces, the potential is limitless.

And my God shall supply all your need according to His riches in glory by Christ Jesus.

Philippians 4:19

Remember that our supply is according to His riches in glory. In His glory, He is unlimited; therefore, there is no limit to the supply of His Spirit.

Chapter 1

The Reservoir

In our modern water supply system, there are several structures that are necessary to provide people with clean, useable water. Some of these structures are useful in illustrating how God's power is supplied in the spirit realm. One such structure is a reservoir. A reservoir is a holding area where water is confined by a dam. It's necessary because it provides a way to control and continue the release of water during periods of drought. In the same way that water is collected and stored for later, we as God's children function as reservoirs of the Holy Spirit. In fact, we're the only conduits of His supply on earth. As we release this treasure stored within, others will experience the power of God during times of spiritual drought. It does seem unusual that God would choose imperfect human vessels to store up and release His power, but the reason He did, is so that others would know that the power is really from Him:

> **However, we possess this precious treasure [the divine Light of the Gospel] in [frail, human] vessels of earth, that the grandeur and exceeding greatness of the power may be shown to be from God and not from ourselves.**
>
> **2 Corinthians 4:7 (AMP)**

The Dam

To avoid excessive water loss from the reservoir, a dam is necessary. The dam must be made of a substance impervious to water. It must be constructed in such a way as to withstand the forces exerted on it. Some forces that engineers must consider when designing a dam are: gravity, hydrostatic pressure (from water behind the dam), uplifts, ice pressures, and earth stress and tension, including the effects of earthquakes.

In the spirit realm, we are responsible for keeping and releasing God's anointed Word to destroy adverse conditions. But just like the force of gravity against the dam, the cares of this world pull against us. We face other problems such as temptation and persecution. But like the dam, we have been formed to withstand all of these external forces exerted on us. We have been made internally fit to receive the supply of the Spirit and then to administer the supply to others. Like the engineers who construct the dam, God has reinforced us on the inside so that we have the ability to receive the supply of the Spirit. God has designed us in His image and likeness, to release His full supply through us. We need to be able to direct the flow of the supply of the Spirit according to God's purpose.

Then Samuel took a flask of oil and poured it on his head, and kissed him and said: "Is it not because the LORD has anointed you commander over His inheritance?

1 Samuel 10:1

When Samuel did this, God had already called Saul and separated him unto Himself. All Samuel was doing by pouring the oil upon his head, was confirming what the Lord had already set into place within Saul's life.

The parable of the sower provides a picture of the external forces that are exerted against us. The deceitfulness of riches and the cares of this world all work together in an attempt to clog the spillways coming from the dam.

"Therefore hear the parable of the sower:

"When anyone hears the word of the kingdom, and does not understand it, then the wicked one comes and snatches away what was sown in his heart. This is he who received seed by the wayside.

"But he who received the seed on stony places, this is he who hears the word and immediately receives it with joy;

"yet he has no root in himself, but endures only for a while. For when tribulation or persecution arises because of the word, immediately he stumbles.

"Now he who received seed among the thorns is he who hears the word, and the cares of this world and the deceitfulness of riches choke the word, and he becomes unfruitful.

"But he who received seed on the good ground is he who hears the word and understands it, who indeed bears fruit and produces: some a hundredfold, some sixty, some thirty."

Matthew 13:18-23

Who shall separate us from the love of Christ? Shall tribulation, or distress, or persecution, or famine, or nakedness, or peril, or sword?

As it is written: "For Your sake we are killed all day long; we are accounted as sheep for the slaughter."

Yet in all these things we are more than conquerors through Him who loved us.

For I am persuaded that neither death nor life, nor angels nor principalities nor powers, nor things present nor things to come,

Nor height nor depth, nor any other created thing, shall be able to separate us from the love of God which is in Christ Jesus our Lord.

Romans 8:35-39

Overflow

After the normal operating water level has been established, means are taken to ensure that this level will not be exceeded. A spillway is therefore necessary to discharge overflow without damage to the dam, powerhouse, or riverbed below the dam. In addition to spillways, outlets are necessary so that water can be drawn continuously from the reservoir. The water is then discharged into the river below the dam and either runs through generators to provide hydroelectric power, or it might be used for irrigation. Look carefully at the following scriptures in relation to what has just been said.

But you, beloved, building yourselves up on your most holy faith, praying in the Holy Spirit,

keep yourselves in the love of God, looking for the mercy of our Lord Jesus Christ unto eternal life.

Jude 20,21

As you therefore have received Christ Jesus the Lord, so walk in Him,

rooted and built up in Him and established in the faith, as you have been taught, abounding in it with thanksgiving.

Colossians 2:6,7

You must build a dam to handle a certain capacity of water. The larger the dam, the greater the capacity of water that can be held, and a greater capacity of energy can then be reproduced.

John G Lake said, "The wonderful measure that the human being is capable of receiving God is demonstrated by some of the incidents in the Word of God. For instance, the most remarkable in scriptures is the transfiguration of Jesus Himself, where, with Peter, James, and John, the Spirit of God came upon Him so powerfully that it radiated out through His being until His clothes became white and glistening and His face shown as the light."[1]

So in this perspective, God has set up a structure which He desires to absolutely possess, Jesus the second Adam and first begotten (prototype) of many sons and daughters.

---

[1]John G. Lake, *John G. Lake* (Kenneth Copeland Publications,1994), p. 25.

Chapter 2
Supply and Demand

When the dam is opened up, it will supply the correct amount of water for its intended purpose. One day while meditating on this, the Lord spoke to me and said: "My supply is like a flood, and there is no lack in it. Whatever you need will be available according to your capacity to believe Me, and your capacity is increased as self gets out of the way."

I have found that prayer, praise, and worship are the greatest tools for crucifying the flesh, but they are also an excellent tool for God to use as a vessel to enable us to be fit to pour His glory through. A watercourse is created when a person spends time in spontaneous praise and worship from the depths of one's heart.

"Who has divided a channel for the overflowing water, or a path for the thunderbolt."

Job 38:25

The Master can give you that which will satisfy. He has in Himself just what you need in this hour. He knows your greater need. You need the blessed Holy Ghost, not merely to satisfy your thirst, but to satisfy the needs of thirsty ones everywhere. For as the blessed Holy Spirit flows through you like rivers of living water, these floods will break what needs to be broken. They will bring to death that which should be brought to death, *but they will bring life and fruit where there is none.*

Smith Wigglesworth said, "What do you have? A well of water? That is good as far as it goes. But Christ wants to see a plentiful supply of the river of the Holy Ghost flowing through you. Here, on this last day of the feast, we find Him preparing them for the Pentecostal fullness that was to come, the fullness that He would shed forth from the glory after His ascension."[1]

The River's Supply

The supply of God's spirit is vaster than an ocean is deep and wide. In the Scripture below God is telling all who are thirsty to come to the waters and drink. This word *water* in Hebrew means: flood or spring. God is telling the thirsty to come to His spring of waters and He will quench their thirst. God is promising to satisfy us with His abundance.

"Ho! Everyone who thirsts, come to the waters; and you who have no money, come, buy and eat....

Why do you spend money for what is not bread, and your wages for what does not satisfy? Listen carefully to Me, and eat what is good, and let your soul delight itself in abundance."

Isaiah 55:1,2

In order for God to fill us, we must place *a demand* on the supply of His Spirit. This is done by being hungry and thirsty for righteousness, by humbling ourselves under the mighty hand of God, by not compromising or settling for less than God's best and by ministering out the supply to others. There are several different ways to put a demand on the supply of the Spirit.

After this, Jesus, knowing that all things were now accomplished, that the Scripture might be fulfilled, said, "I thirst!"

John 19:28

When we give out of our spirit to someone else we are giving out of the supply of the spirit within us. Once we do this, we have to be refilled. When Jesus hung on the cross, everything in Him was given out in order to supply us with redemption. He had nothing left in Himself to give. Many times in ministering to others we may experience a feeling of emptiness afterwards. That's because we have not yielded ourselves completely to the supply of the Spirit. We need to go back to the waters and fill up our supply again. A lot of people don't realize this and may feel like they're discouraged after a meeting where the supply of the Spirit was manifested through them to others. They just need to be refilled with the supply of the Spirit. Have another drink!

On the last day, that great day of the feast, Jesus stood and cried out, saying, "If anyone thirsts, let him come to Me and drink.

"He who believes in Me, as the Scripture has said, out of his heart will flow rivers of living water."

John 7:37,38

God's desire is for us to be so full that our spillway flows to others and our outlets draw water continuously from the reservoir, which needs to be supplied each day with fresh living water. A spillway provides water for rivers and lakes. It controls the amount of water going into the river or lake. It can also take water out, if the water level gets too high. This is what happens with us; we have a river flowing forth from us. We can manage the amount of water that flows out of us to others; or we can allow God to manage how much spills from within us.

God provides us with the means and power to water or irrigate those around us. This may seem drastic to some, but there is overflow. When the detachment of troops came to get Jesus in the Garden of Gethsemane there was so much of God in His Son Jesus that when they said they were seeking "Jesus of Nazareth," and Jesus said, "I am He," they drew back and fell to the ground. There was so much of the supply of the presence of God within Him that when He declared who He was, the power within Him could not contain itself at those words. I pray that we will come to such a great depth of consciousness that we are truly children of the Most High God, that the supply which God desires to release through us will be given free course in our lives.

I've seen many instances while praying for someone, where the ushers and everyone around the person I was praying for, all experienced the overflow of the anointing. While praying for them, the anointing overflowed onto those around them, and before you know it there was a whole group of people lying around on the floor touched by the power of God.

The supply of the Spirit flows out of us in rivers of living water. We can clearly see in the above verses that when thirst is fulfilled, we become a river of life flowing out to those in need. In Revelation 22:1, we see an excellent example of this river that flows out of us. It's interesting that the word "river" in Greek means: "a current, brook, *drinkable running water*, flood, river, or stream.

And he showed me a pure river of water of life, clear as crystal, proceeding from the throne of God and of the Lamb.

Revelation 22:1

The river comes from the throne of God into our inner most being, and it must continue to come out of our bellies. It's the anchor that's tied behind the veil in the presence of God, and we have a spiritual umbilical cord. In the natural, our umbilical cord was cut at birth, but when we were saved, we have a spiritual umbilical cord that developed inside of us that reaches into the Holiest of Holies, into the presence of God. Just as a baby in the natural receives all of its nutrients, all of it's food, all of its life source through the umbilical cord, so are we to receive all of our life source, all that we need from Him. God wants creative things to be birthed through us.

"River, river, river deep within, rise up, rise up, rise up within. Flow, flow, flow, do not stop, but go for this river," says the Lord.

The throne is symbolic of the throne that God has set up within our hearts. The river flows forth from the throne of our hearts. I'm reminded of another song that goes like this, "There is a river that flows from deep within. There is a fountain that cleanses from all sin. Come to this water there is a vast supply. There is a river that never shall run dry." GLORY!! I don't know about you, but I personally want an unlimited supply of all that belongs to me as a child of God.

---

[1]Wayne Warner, *The Anointing of His Spirit* (Servant Publications, 1994), p.134.

Chapter 3

The Source of the Supply

In this chapter, we will look at God our Father as the source of the supply of the Spirit.

The Father

Every good gift and every perfect (free, large, full) gift is from above; it comes down from the Father of all [that gives] light, in [the shining of] Whom there can be no variation [rising or setting] or shadow cast by His turning [as in an eclipse].

James 1:17 (AMP)

What is the point of origin for every good and perfect gift? Where does the anointing, the love and the power which we have available as Christians begin to flow from? They flow from the Father. Remember there are things that you will never receive or understand about your Father until you draw near to Him.

If anyone speaks, let him speak as the oracles of God. If anyone ministers, let him do it as with the ability which God supplies, that in all things God may be glorified through Jesus Christ, to whom belong the glory and the dominion forever and ever. Amen.

1 Peter 4:11

When any one is endeavoring to serve others, let him do so in reliance on the strength which God supplies.

1 Peter 4:11 (TCNT)

Our heavenly Father is the source of everything. He is the One from whom our resources, strength, and power originate. The only issue for Him has been finding someone willing to believe and receive His supply. Notice the first part of this verse from the Gospel of John:

For even as the Father has life in Himself and is self-existent, so He has given to the Son to have life in Himself and be self-existent.

John 5:26 (AMP)

For the Father, being as He is the source of life; has made the Son the source of life....

John 5:26 (Rieu)

God has life in Himself and is self existent because God is life. There is no life of any kind that does not originate from and is not sustained by God.

Light

In the creation of physical life, we find God as the source of the power at work through the creation of light. Power is measured at the speed of light. Sixteen billion two hundred and forty million miles were created in 24 hours when God said, "Let there be light." That same power resides on the inside of us!

For with You [God] is the fountain of life; in Your [God's] light do we see light.

Psalm 36:9 (AMP)

For the source of life itself springs from You (God); we shall increase in wisdom as You (God) enlighten us.

Psalm 36:9 (Har)

It is an interesting fact that many scientists (both Christian and non-Christian) believe that all matter originated from some form of light energy. This is not surprising because in one sense, God's life and light are synonymous. The relationship is even more obvious when it comes to the spiritual aspect. This is the energy source from which all supply originates.

In Him was life, and the life was the light of men.

And the light shines in the darkness and the darkness did not comprehended it.

John 1:4,5

His life is the light that shines through the darkness — and the darkness can never extinguish it.

John 1:5 (Tay)

Although the darkness may certainly try, it cannot comprehend the light. Comprehend means to seize, lay hold, or possess. Darkness will not be able to seize us, lay hold of us, or possess us! In fact, the hidden things of darkness will be revealed, as there will be no place for darkness to hide in the light of God's Word.

Your word is a lamp to my feet and a light to my path.

Psalm 119:105

God's Word is a lamp unto our feet, so everywhere we walk, darkness will be revealed. Therefore we are destroying the devil's devices through the supply of the Spirit.

15

The Father's Children

"Or what man is there among you who, if his son asks for bread, will give him a stone?

"Or if he asks for a fish, will give him a serpent?

"If you then, being evil, know how to give good gifts to your children, how much more will your Father who is in heaven give good things to those who ask Him!

Matthew 7:9-11

God wants us to have a full revelation of what it means to have Him as our Father. He wants us to take full advantage of our privileges as His children in the kingdom He has given us dominion over.

Blessed be the God and Father of our Lord Jesus Christ, who has blessed us with every spiritual blessing in the heavenly places in Christ.

Ephesians 1:3

When we were children and living in our earthly father's house, we enjoyed the shelter and lived on the food that he provided. At times, we may have even driven the car for which He provides the gas. Just as those resources came from our earthly father, how much more will God provide? It is evident from scripture that one of Jesus' priorities in teaching the people was to get this revelation across to them that God was the source of their supply.

For every beast of the forest is mine, and the cattle upon a thousand hills.

If I were hungry, I would not tell thee: for the world is mine, and the fullness thereof.

Psalm 50:10,12 (KJV)

16

When people make the statement, "I don't have enough, I can't afford this," they're setting themselves up as the source of their supply. God said that He is Jehovah El Shaddai, Jehovah Jireh. He is the All-Sufficient One; therefore, I am sufficient with My Father's sufficiency. Through Jesus, we have access to the source of the supply of the Spirit, which comes from God, to bring all that is needed according to the riches in His glory.

Chapter 4
Accessing the Supply

Access Defined

First, I believe it is important that we understand what access means. In the *Webster's 1828 Dictionary* access is defined as:

1. A coming to; near approach; admittance; admission; as to gain access to a prince.

2. Approach or the way by which a thing may be approached; as, the access to is by a neck of land.

3. Means of approach; liberty to approach; implying previous obstacles.

4. Addition; increase by something added; as an access of territory.[1]

Therefore, having been justified by faith, we have peace with God through our Lord Jesus Christ,

through whom we also have access by faith into this grace in which we stand, and rejoice in hope of the glory of God.
                                                  Romans 5:1,2

For through Him we both have access by one Spirit to the Father.
                                                  Ephesians 2:18

The Greek word for access is prosago: to lead towards, i.e. (transitively) to conduct near (summon, present), or (intransitively) to approach — bring, draw near.

Thank the Lord that through Christ, the author and finisher of faith, we can access the same Spirit.

The Son

All things were made through Him, and without Him nothing was made that was made.

John 1:3

And He is before all things, and in Him all things consist.

Colossians 1:17

The *Son* demonstrates how to access the supply of the Spirit. He is the administrator of the supply. An administrator is one who manages the supply to direct it to the point of need. When Jesus became the Mediator of a better covenant, He became the administrator of God's supply. He now sits at the right hand of the Father, administrating the supply of the Spirit on our behalf.

For there is one God and one Mediator between God and men, the Man Christ Jesus.

1 Timothy 2:5

But now He has obtained a more excellent ministry, inasmuch as He is also Mediator of a better covenant, which was established on better promises.

Hebrews 8:6

Through the blood of Jesus we have access to God, the source. When Jesus was on the earth he showed us how to access the source of the supply. Jesus showed us the Father and became the avenue for the supply of the spirit to us. By the supply of the spirit within us, we are now the avenue with which Jesus is able to show the fullness of the Father to those in need of Him. We become more than a channel for the supply of the Spirit much like the irrigation channel mentioned in the previous chapters, this happened when the kingdom of God came upon us.

Phillip said to Him, "Lord show us the Father, and it is sufficient for us."

Jesus said to him, "Have I been with you so long, and yet you have not known Me, Phillip? He who has seen Me has seen the Father; so how can you say, 'Show us the Father?'"

John 14:8,9

For in Him dwells all the fullness of the God- head bodily.

Colossians 2:9

In Christ there is all of God in a human body.

Colossians 2:9 (Tay)

Not only has God placed His very own life within His Son Jesus Christ, He has also filled Him with the very essence of His godly nature and has placed it within us.

The Fullness

Think about this for a moment. In Christ dwells all the fullness of the Godhead bodily. All of the things that make up the fullness of God, His omnipotence, His omniscience, all these are residing in the anointing of God. His power, strength, and the supply of His Spirit are in Christ, the Anointed One and His Anointing. Everything that we could possibly need in this life and the one to come can be found in Christ, the Anointed One and His Anointing. Notice that the verse states "In Christ dwells *all* the fullness of the Godhead bodily." *All* the fullness means an unlimited supply. In Jesus Christ (God's anointed Son), lies an unlimited source of God's power. Why did God invest so much in His Son? So

21

that we, as His children, could have a channel to partake or "drink" from. In one sense we could say that Christ is the channel for the fullness to come to us.

Smith Wigglesworth said, "God has designed it, in the pavilion of His splendor with the majesty of His glory, he comes, and touching human weakness, beautifies it in the Spirit of Holiness until the affectiveness of this wonderful sonship is made manifest in us till we all become the embodiment of the fullness of Christ. "[2]

Maturing in Christ

For out of His fullness (abundance) we have all received [all had a share and we were all supplied with] one grace after another and spiritual blessing upon spiritual blessing and even favor and gift [heaped] upon gift.

For while the Law was given through Moses, grace (unearned, undeserved favor and spiritual blessing) and truth came through Jesus Christ.

John 1:16,17 (AMP)

As was mentioned before, "In Christ dwells all the fullness of the Godhead bodily." If we are complete in Him we don't need anything else. When we access the supply of the Spirit and allow Him to possess us, *His character and personality will find full expression inside us. We are made in His image and likeness.* The more He flows through us, the greater our capacity for releasing His anointing will become. The greater the capacity becomes, the more mature we will become in Him.

Do not forget that our being *mature* is directly tied to our revelation of becoming the manifested sons in Christ's fullness.

The Spirit Himself bears witness with our spirit that we are children of God,

22

And if children then heirs — heirs of God and joint heirs with Christ, if indeed we suffer with Him, that we may also be glorified together.

Romans 8:16,17

If we are his children then we are God's heirs, and all that Christ inherits will belong to all of us as well!...

Romans 8:17 (Phi)

...if we share his sufferings now in order to share His splendor hereafter.

Romans 8:17 (The New English Bible)

by which have been given to us exceedingly great and precious promises, that through these you may be partakers of the divine nature....

2 Peter 1:4

Through the adoption of sons we have become partakers of the kingdom of God. We have been adopted into His kingdom, and therefore, we have been made joint heirs with Christ. We gain access to the supply of the Spirit for our every need as children of God and joint heirs with Christ.

Joint Heirs

What does it mean to be a *joint heir* with Christ? The word joint heir in the Greek, is the word *"sugkleronomos"* a co-heir, i.e. (by analogy) participant in common: fellow (joint) — heir, heir together, heir with. It means that we are in joint inheritance with Him. We are joint partakers, seated in heavenly places with Christ. In one sense we are granted the privilege of approaching and receiving from God's throne. In Christ we are literally standing before the throne room of grace and *"obtaining grace to help in time of need"* (Hebrews 4:16).

Smith Wigglesworth wrote, "When our whole lives are surged by the power of God, we become subjects of the Spirit of the Living God and we are moved by the almightiness of God. Then we live and move and have our being in this flow of God's wonder working power. God is able to make all grace abound towards us."[3]

Abide in the Vine

In this chapter, we're talking about accessing the supply of the Spirit. In order to have access to the supply of the Spirit, we must abide in the vine *continually*. We abide by remaining in the very presence of God. We do this through fellowship with Him, through praise and worship, through a variety of ways. In order to maintain access to the supply of the Spirit, we must be living in *constant unbroken fellowship* with Him.

Even so consider yourselves also dead to sin and your relation to it broken, but alive to God [living in unbroken fellowship with Him] in Christ Jesus.
Romans 6:11 (AMP)

As we stay hooked up to the presence of God, we access the supply of the Spirit. Nehemiah 8:10 says, "the joy of the Lord is our strength." Isaiah 12:3 tells us, "with joy you draw water out of the wells of salvation." This is talking about accessing the supply of the Spirit through joy. In the presence of the Lord is fullness of joy. When we access the supply of the Spirit, we access strength, joy, and every thing we need to stay in His presence. As we abide in His presence, we abide in the vine; as we abide in the vine, we will grow strong and vigorous in the truth that *we act* upon.

"Abide in Me and I in you. As the branch cannot bear fruit of itself, unless it abides in the vine, neither can you, unless you abide in Me."
John 15:4

God is in Christ, and Christ is in us. Just as Christ has the fullness of the Godhead bodily, we have the fullness of the Godhead bodily *dwelling in us.* The supply of the Spirit comes from Christ, the Anointed One and His Anointing. In Him there is *no limit* to our capacity to receive from God, the source of our supply. He wants us to live the enthroned life where we're seated with Him in heavenly places. This is a quality life where we're with Him in the spirit, partaking of His grace, which sets us up to receive the source of His power. We must focus on Jesus Christ as the living channel so that He can be formed in us, thereby making us living channels for the supply of His Spirit.

Behold, I will do a new thing, now it shall spring forth; shall you not know it? I will even make a road in the wilderness and rivers in the desert.

The beast of the field will honor Me, the jackals and the ostriches, because I give waters in the wilderness and rivers in the desert, to give drink to My people, My chosen.
                                          Isaiah 43:19,20

Drinking From the Rock

We must drink from the Rock that is *Christ.* Remember, Christ is in charge of the supply of the Spirit. The supply of the Spirit comes from God *through* Christ. We are drinking from the Rock, which is Christ, the Anointed One. God wants us to have an endless supply of the Spirit. Jesus has now been glorified. There's a river flowing out of Christ. We've been made to drink of the rock of Christ, His anointing, His river that flows from His innermost being. We have been made to drink of the very essence, the very life of God.

And all [of them] ate the same spiritual (supernaturally given) food,

25

And they all drank the same spiritual (supernaturally given) drink. For they drank from a spiritual Rock which followed them [produced by the sole power of God Himself without natural instrumentality], and the Rock was Christ.

1 Corinthians 10:3,4 (AMP)

Before this in Numbers chapter twenty God told Moses to speak to the rock and it would yield water. But Moses struck the rock twice instead of speaking to it.

For by one Spirit we were all baptized into one body — whether Jews or Greeks, whether slaves or free — and have all been made to drink into one Spirit.

1 Corinthians 12:13

Another way to activate a greater flow of the supply of the Spirit is to speak to the gifts and callings within you and command them to come to harvest.

A Continual Flow

In the following scripture, Job recalls the days when the Lord was abundantly releasing His supply to and through him. Job states:

When my steps were bathed with cream, and the rock poured out rivers of oil for me!

Job 29:6

The cream in this scripture is talking about the solid milk or the wealth of the Word. The rivers of oil are the supply of the Spirit. In this last move of God, we'll see a continual flow of the anointing that will never stop.

So what should we be drinking from? Job 29:6 is prophetically speaking of this present day anointing that walks in *rivers* of oil. Oil preserves and serves, it's a point of contact for the abundance of the anointing. This present day anointing does not fall under the Old

Covenant, but under the New Covenant. It's a river that will continually flow.

I once heard Gloria Copeland say, "The anointing is the kingdom of God bursting in upon this natural realm and it brings God's free favors profusely." Profusely means lavishly, literally, extravagantly, over, and abounding.

The following are some examples of drinking in the Bible. I have included them here because of their spiritual significance to the subject. Note in these situations where there was a demand put on the supply of the anointing.

So He came to a city of Samaria which is called Sychar, near the plot of ground that Jacob gave to his son Joseph. [Sychar is the Greek word which is Hebrew in origin and it means strong drink.]

Now Jacob's well was there. Jesus therefore, being wearied from His journey, sat thus by the well. It was about the sixth hour.

A woman of Samaria came to draw water. Jesus said to her, "Give Me a drink."

For His disciples had gone away into the city to buy food.

Then the woman of Samaria said to Him, "How is it that You, being a Jew, ask a drink from me, a Samaritan woman?" For Jews have no dealings with Samaritans.

Jesus answered and said to her, "If you knew the gift of God, and who it is who says to you, 'Give Me a drink,' you would have asked Him, and He would have given you living water."

The woman said to Him, "Sir, You have nothing to draw with, and the well is deep. Where then do You get that living water?

"Are You greater than our father Jacob, who gave us the well, and drank from it himself, as well as his sons and his livestock?"

Jesus answered and said to her, "Whoever drinks of this water will thirst again,

"but whoever drinks of the water that I shall give him will never thirst. But the water that I shall give him will become in him a fountain of water springing up into everlasting life."

The woman said to Him, "Sir, give me this water, that I may not thirst, nor come here to draw."

John 4:5-15

The woman at the well came to Jesus and said give me a drink of this water that you speak of so I may never be thirsty again. If you notice, the first person in this story to ask for a drink was Jesus. When she placed a demand on the anointing that was on Jesus' life, guess what happened? The demand that she placed on Him caused Him to have a word of knowledge about the situation that she was in at that time. Jesus began to read her mail. That was a word of knowledge. He was beginning to give her a drink. When she placed a demand on the anointing, it activated the gifts of the Spirit. You can pull things out of people that have never been there before.

When I hold revivals, I tell the people to raise their hands and pull them down towards them and say, "Jesus." When they do this, they are pulling on the anointing. When we do this, we're placing a demand on the gifts so that the anointing can flow in order for the glory of God to fill the place. That brings in the supply of the Spirit. It draws in what the Spirit wants to supply and brings it to completion and fulfillment.

Many times when praying for someone I'll command them to laugh, and they'll ask, "Why must I laugh?" The answer to this question is, it's time to give Jesus a drink. He wants a drink of us.

Jesus answered and said to her, "Whosoever drinks of this water will thirst again, but whoever drinks of the water that I shall give him will never thirst. But the water that I shall give him will become in him a fountain of water springing up into everlasting life" (John 4:13,14). Access to this fountain was made when word of knowledge was given concerning her husbands.

Give Me a Drink

Now Abraham was old, well advanced in age; and the LORD had blessed Abraham in all things.

So Abraham said to the oldest servant of his house, who ruled over all that he had, "Please, put your hand under my thigh,

"and I will make you swear by the LORD, the God of heaven and the God of the earth, that you will not take a wife for my son from the daughters of the Canaanites, among whom I dwell;

"but you shall go to my country and to my family, and take a wife for my son Isaac."

And the servant said to him, "Perhaps the woman will not be willing to follow me to this land. Must I take your son back to the land from which you came?"

But Abraham said to him, "Beware that you do not take my son back there.

"The LORD God of heaven, who took me from my father's house and from the land of my family, and who spoke to me and swore to me, saying, 'To your descendants I give this land,' He will send

His angel before you, and you shall take a wife for my son from there.

"And if the woman is not willing to follow you, then you will be released from this oath; only do not take my son back there."

So the servant put his hand under the thigh of Abraham his master, and swore to him concerning this matter.

Then the servant took ten of his master's camels and departed, for all his master's goods were in his hand. And he arose and went to Mesopotamia, to the city of Nahor.

And he made his camels kneel down outside the city by a well of water at evening time, the time when women go out to draw water.

Then he said, "O LORD God of my master Abraham, please give me success this day, and show kindness to my master Abraham.

"Behold, here I stand by the well of water, and the daughters of the men of the city are coming out to draw water.

"Now let it be that the young woman to whom I say, 'Please let down your pitcher that I may drink,' and she says, 'Drink, and I will also give your camels a drink' — let her be the one You have appointed for Your servant Isaac. And by this I will know that You have shown kindness to my master."

Genesis 24:1-14

The servant has been sent out to look for a wife for Isaac. Now Isaac means laughter. The servant of Isaac is going to ask for a drink. He is representing Isaac and Isaac is saying give me a drink. The one to whom he says, "Give me a drink," let that one be my wife.

And the servant ran to meet her and said, "Please let me drink a little water from your pitcher."

So she said, "Drink, my lord." Then she quickly let her pitcher down to her hand, and gave him a drink.

And when she had finished giving him a drink, she said, "I will draw water for your camels also, until they have finished drinking."

Then she quickly emptied her pitcher into the trough, ran back to the well to draw water, and drew for all his camels.

Genesis 24:17-20

The servant came along and placed a demand. The woman who answered that demand and gave him a drink would become Isaac's wife. Isaac is laughter. Isaac represents wells. It represents rivers flowing. The Philistines came along and tried to plug up Isaac's wells. The Philistines represent all different kinds of sins. This represents the devil trying to come along and plug up your wells. Notice verses 20 and 21 of Genesis 26.

Also Isaac's servants dug in the valley, and found a well of running water there.

But the herdsmen of Gerar quarreled with Isaac's herdsmen, saying, "The water is ours." So he called the name of the well Esek, because they quarreled with him.

Then they dug another well, and they quarreled over that one also. So he called its name Sitnah.

Genesis 26:19-21

When researching these two verses, I found it interesting to find that the word Esek means strife and the word Sitnah means opposition and accusation. Strife and accusation will plug up your wells. It's just more dirt in the well. It's also interesting to note the meaning of the valley of Gerar, which means to drag off roughly, to destroy. Laughter pitched his tent in the enemies territory and began to take possession with laughter.

Isaac means laughter. Sarah said that the Lord had made her to laugh. Isaac went out and sowed in the land, and he reaped a hundred fold. Laughter was sown in the land, and laughter reaped a hundred fold. As Isaac went through his life, the laughter followed him. When he went to find his wife, they had to find the woman that would come and offer his servant a drink. When laughter saw the woman, laughter said, "Give me a drink."

Now the Philistines had stopped up all the wells which his father's servants had dug in the days of Abraham his father, and they had filled them with earth.

And Abimelech said to Isaac, "Go away from us, for you are much mightier than we."

Then Isaac departed from there and pitched his tent in the Valley of Gerar, and dwelt there.

And Isaac dug again the wells of water which they had dug in the days of Abraham his father, for the Philistines had stopped them up after the death of Abraham. He called them by the names, which his father had called them.

Genesis 26:15-18

The Philistines plugged up the wells and laughter came along and dug up the wells. I've seen people lie on the ground laughing and all the while the demons are leaving them.

The first person who asked for a drink in this story to get a wife was Isaac. Laughter placed a demand on the woman at the well and said give me a drink. When she gave him a drink, she became the bride of laughter. Jesus comes in John chapter four, and says to the woman at the well, "give Me a drink." Who placed the demand? Jesus did, but who really has the laughter? Who really has the springs and fountains that want to flow? Jesus does. Jesus is coming into your life and is doing the same thing. He's saying the same thing. Give Me a drink. Do you know what He's doing? He's pushing a button inside of you to see if you're going to recognize and respond and say, *"I want that living water."* If you had known who it was that was asking you for a drink, you would have asked Him to give you living water, because He wants to bring a fountain out of you.

God wants to bring a supply of the Spirit that will meet every need you have, that will unplug the wells of the Philistines and that will bring healing and strength to your body. In this story, you see the demand being placed on the fountain within and letting it come forth. When the joy of the Lord is your strength, you won't be weak and depressed. If you hunger and thirst after righteousness, you shall be filled.

When he came to Lehi, the Philistines came shouting against him. Then the Spirit of the LORD came mightily upon him; and the ropes that were on his arms became like flax that is burned with fire, and his bonds broke loose from his hands.

Judges 15:14

The anointing burns the bondages of the devil in pieces.

He found a fresh jawbone of a donkey, reached out his hand and took it, and killed a thousand men with it.

Judges 15:15

Samson begins to brag. Here he's singing a song full of pride and ego. I thought that God did it. Pride will stop you.

Then Samson said: "With the jawbone of a donkey, heaps upon heaps, with the jawbone of a donkey I have slain a thousand men!"

And so it was, when he had finished speaking, that he threw the jawbone from his hand, and called that place Ramath Lehi.

Judges 15:16,17

Ramath Lehi means a seat of idolatry, the high place. He renamed Lehi the seat of idolatry or in other words, the place of bragging. 7413 ramah (raw-maw'); feminine active participle of 7311; a height (as a seat of idolatry): KJV — high place.

Then he became very thirsty; so he cried out to the LORD and said, "You have given this great deliverance by the hand of Your servant; and now shall I die of thirst and fall into the hand of the uncircumcised?"

Judges 15:18

I thought that he just said that he did it all by himself. Wasn't he just bragging in the scripture verse before that he did it all by himself. Now when he's thirsty and he's about to die, he starts acknowledging that it was God. Two scriptures before he was singing a pride song. He even calls himself a servant after just singing a pride song.

So God split the hollow place that is in Lehi, and water came out, and he drank; and his spirit returned, and he revived. Therefore he called its name En Hakkore, which is in Lehi to this day.

Judges 15:19

God supplied a miracle for proud Samson. The word En Hakkore in the Hebrew means a spring for the

34

caller. Samson had to acknowledge God's Lordship, and place a demand on the Spirit of God. There is a spring for the caller, if you call out to God and say, "I am thirsty."

David said, "As a deer pants after the water, so my soul longs for you." Sometimes he talks about being thirsty and dry like he's in the wilderness and can't get his thirst quenched. We need to come to the place where we are thirsty. We need to be absolutely thirsty for the presence of God. If you want God to unlock a spring within you, then you need to place a demand.

I believe the word En Hakkore (a spring for the caller) to Cyrus, king of Persia, in the following verse, shows the liberty to place a great demand upon the supply of the Spirit.

"Thus says the LORD to His anointed, to Cyrus, whose right hand I have held..."

Thus says the Lord, the Holy One of Israel, and His Maker: "Ask Me of things to come concerning My sons; and concerning the work of My hands, you command Me."

Isaiah 45:1,11

I believe that this scripture shows that God wants you to know what belongs to us as sons and daughters of God. He wants you to know how to place a demand upon that supply that He has made available to you through His Spirit.

Samson is a type of the church. When Samson allowed himself to be lured to sleep by Delilah, she cut off his hair. The length of his hair represented the supply of the Spirit in his life. So when the hair was cut off, so was the supply of the Spirit. When the church plays games with the world, they're cutting off the supply of the Spirit. When the hair is cut, the anointing (the supply of the Spirit) is cut off. But now the hair is growing back and the supply of the Spirit grows stronger.

Making Space for the Supply

So Jesus went with him, and a great multitude followed Him and thronged Him.

Now a certain woman had a flow of blood for twelve years,

and had suffered many things from many physicians. She had spent all that she had and was no better, but rather grew worse.

When she heard about Jesus, she came behind Him in the crowd and touched His garment.

Mark 5:24-27

The first thing that you have to do is hear about Jesus. Faith comes by hearing and hearing by the Word of God.

For she said, "If only I may touch His clothes, I shall be made well."

Immediately the fountain of her blood was dried up, and she felt in her body that she was healed of the affliction.

And Jesus, immediately knowing in Himself that power had gone out of Him, turned around in the crowd and said, "Who touched My clothes?"

But His disciples said to Him, "You see the multitude thronging You, and You say, 'Who touched Me?'"

And He looked around to see her who had done this thing.

But the woman, fearing and trembling, knowing what had happened to her, came and fell down before Him and told Him the whole truth.

36

And He said to her, "Daughter, your faith has made you well. Go in peace, and be healed of your affliction."

Mark 5:28-34

You see here that faith met virtue. Jesus turned around knowing that dunamis, explosive power left Him, because anointing was flowing out of Him. Did the anointing heal her? Not really, because Jesus said her faith had made her whole. We see two things here. Faith placed a demand on the anointing, but when the anointing and faith came together she had a miracle. When faith meets the anointing you'll have a miracle. I can be anointed and say I feel power when I move my hands. I can feel the tangible presence of the Holy Ghost. I can feel power, but if you don't have faith, you won't have a miracle unless the gifts of miracles and healing are flowing. There are times that you can be healed just because you know that if you have the brother lay hands on you, the healing anointing is going to flow through your body and you'll have a miracle. That's the supply of the Spirit.

We see several things about this woman. Number one, she came. You have to come to the place where healing is flowing. You have to come to the place where there's a miracle worker. The second thing that she did was, she "heard." Faith comes by hearing and hearing by the Word of God. The third thing that she did was, she said, "If I may but touch His garment, I will be made whole." What are you saying? The Bible says if you say to the mountain, "Be removed and be cast into the sea," and do not doubt in your heart, but believe those things which you say when you say them, they will come to pass. So what are you saying about your healing? Are you speaking life or death about your healing? The fourth thing that she did was, she moved forward. She had to act. She had to move. She had to press forward. She had to reach up into heaven and say, "I praise you, Jesus, that I am healed." You need to say it. You need to do it. You need to receive it; and you need to tell it. (1) You have to come to where faith is. (2) You have to hear faith. (3) You have to say and speak faith. (4) You have to do something about it, and…(5) you have to receive it. That's placing a demand on the supply of the Spirit. Whatever you need, you have to press in and say, "I receive, it Lord. I accept it, Lord."

When the anointing goes into your body, it immediately begins to work. Your body is the temple of the Holy Ghost, and you need to let it affect your soul. You need to let it affect your outer court. The veil has been removed in Christ. He wants to blow away your soul. You need to let the anointing manifest in your flesh. We are spirit, soul, and body. Doesn't Jesus the Healer live in you? Then you need to yield to Jesus the Healer. You need to let Him manifest in your flesh, because then you will be the one administering the healing. The Lord sits in the heavens and laughs.

The Bible says in Psalm 126, we were like them that dreamed; then was our mouth filled with laughter and our tongue with singing. For we were like captives in Zion, but now we are free. When you are free, then your tongue is filled with laughter. Laughter will unplug all of the gook. It will open up the cholesterol veins and unplug those arteries. You and I need to pursue the hunger of God. And we all need to press in and say, "I thank you, Father, that I'm drinking from the fountain. I'm drinking from the rivers that flow from above. My soul is anchored in heaven and I'm receiving my nutrients and supply straight from the rivers that flow from beneath that throne. Out of my belly will flow forth rivers of living water." You need to live attached to heaven just as a baby is attached to the womb. Our lives are hidden with Christ in God (Colossians 3). If you're in hiding with Christ in God, what better hiding place could you have? Nothing can touch you when you hide with Christ in God.

Channels for Irrigation

In order for us to fill others, we must be filled ourselves. A good way to look at this is to study the meaning and process of irrigation. Irrigation is a means of watering land to sustain plant growth in areas of irregular rainfall. Irrigation is used during dry spells to ensure harvests and to increase crop yields. Irrigated land produces over twice the yield of non-irrigated fields. Irrigation has greatly expanded the amount of usable land and the production of food throughout the world.

In order for God's Spirit within to flow out to others, we must allow the Holy Spirit to establish the irrigation channel within us. It must fill us to overflowing, thus watering the incorruptible seed of the Word in our hearts and producing a rich harvest in our lives and the lives of others around us. When we allow the Holy Spirit to irrigate our lives with the water of His Word, we're able to be a channel of irrigation for others around us, thus enabling the Word to be harvested in their lives.

Strengthen the weak hands, and make firm the feeble knees.

Say to those who are fearful-hearted, "Be strong, do not fear! Behold, your God will come with vengeance, with the recompense of God; He will come and save you."

Then the eyes of the blind shall be opened, and the ears of the deaf shall be unstopped.

Then the lame shall leap like a deer, and the tongue of the dumb sing. For waters shall burst forth in the wilderness, and streams in the desert.

The parched ground shall become a pool, and the thirsty land springs of water; in the habitation of the jackals, where each lay, there shall be grass with reeds and rushes.

Isaiah 35:3-7

Lord, I pray, let Your waters burst forth out of our lives.

---

[1] *American Dictionary* (B.J.C. Merriam Co., 1828).

[2] Warner, p. 85.

[3] Warner, p. 218.

Chapter 5
The Holy Spirit

Endued With Power

"**A**nd the glory which You gave Me I have given them, that they may be one just as We are one."

John 17:22

Glory can also be described as the spirit without measure.

"**For He whom God has sent speaks the words of God, for God does not give the Spirit by measure.**

"**The Father loves the Son, and has given all things into His hand**"

John 3:34,35

How did the Father send Jesus? Jesus came with everything He needed to complete His task; He had the spirit without measure. Jesus prays that we are sent the same way:

So Jesus said to them again, "Peace to you! As the Father has sent Me, I also send you."

John 20:21

"**Behold, I send *the Promise of My Father* upon you; but tarry in the city of Jerusalem until you are endued with power from on high.**"

(Amplified — clothed with power from on high)

Luke 24:49

Until you have been invested with power from above.

Luke 24:49 (TCNT)

"...until you are armed with the power from above."

Luke 24:49 (NEB)

But you shall receive power (ability, efficiency, and might) *when the Holy Spirit has come upon you,* **and you shall be My witnesses in Jerusalem and all Judea and Samaria and to the ends (the very bounds) of the earth.**

Acts 1:8 (AMP)

Jesus instructed His disciples to wait for the power they needed to be witnesses. When the Holy Spirit came upon them, they received that power. Naturally, we also need to be endued with power from on high and receive the same supply of the Spirit. God's design was to supply us with it as soon as Jesus was exalted:

"Therefore being exalted to the right hand of God, and having received from the Father the promise of the Holy Spirit, He poured out this which you now see and hear."

Acts 2:33

But the Comforter (Counselor, Helper, Intercessor, Advocate, Strengthener, Standby), the Holy Spirit, Whom the Father will send in My name [in My place, to represent Me and act on My behalf], He will teach you all things. And He will cause you to recall (will remind you of, bring to your remembrance) everything I have told you.

John 14:26 (AMP)

Not only will He pour out His Spirit on us, He will teach us all things and bring all things to our remembrance. This is a key to understanding the flow of the supply of the Spirit.

In Him you also who have heard the Word of Truth, the glad tidings (Gospel) of your salvation, and have believed in and adhered to and relied on Him, were stamped with the seal of the long-promised Holy Spirit.

That [Spirit] is the guarantee of our inheritance [the first fruits, the pledge and foretaste, the down payment on our heritage], in anticipation of its full redemption and our acquiring [complete] possession of it — to the praise of His glory.

Ephesians 1:13,14 (AMP)

In this manner we are partaking or sharing in His anointing. Since this is the case, what tangible manifestations should we be experiencing? How did God confirm His anointing on Jesus?

You men of Israel, listen to what I have to say: Jesus of Nazareth, a Man accredited and pointed out and shown forth and commended and attested to you by God by the mighty works and [the power of performing] wonders and signs which God worked through Him [right] in your midst, as you yourselves know.

Acts 2:22 (AMP)

God confirmed Jesus' calling by performing signs and wonders through Him. He was literally the channel for the supply of God's power to flow through. It was God's intention to demonstrate His power through Christ, the Anointed One and then to transfer that power to us. How does He do this?

My little children, for whom I am again suffering birth pangs *until Christ is completely and permanently formed (molded) within you!*

Galatians 4:19 (AMP)

My dear children, who for whom I am again enduring a mother's pains, till a likeness of Christ shall have been formed in you.

Galatians 4:19 (TCNT)

He wants the Anointed One, along with His access to the fullness of God, to be formed in our inner man. We need to believe for the virtue of the Lord to be so manifested through our bodies that as we touch people, they are healed. We need to believe for the supply of the Spirit to flow through us to others.

John G. Lake said, "The ministry of the Christian is the ministry of the Spirit. If the Christian cannot minister the Spirit of God, in the true sense then He is not a Christian."[1]

The anointing flowing through the anointed ones of God is what will reveal to others the true character of Christianity.

And just as we have borne the image [of the man] of dust, so shall we and so let *us also bear the image [of the Man] of heaven.*

1 Corinthians 15:49 (AMP)

...so we shall wear the likeness of the heavenly man.

1 Corinthians 15:49 (NEB)

Access Through Prayer

By being sealed with the Holy Spirit of Promise, we are guaranteed to have access to the supply of the Spirit to flow and minister through us. Prayer is vital to accessing the supply of the Spirit. Prayer brings a consistent movement of the Holy Spirit to produce the end-time increase. When we pray, we access the supply of the Spirit because we become more and more conscious of the presence of God in our spirit, soul, and body. Thus it enables us to become more conscious of the outpouring of His Spirit from us to others. As a result, there will be an increase in the inner supply of the Spirit. But without prayer there is no fullness of the Spirit. Without prayer there will be no supply of the Spirit available.

We see in the book of Acts the importance of praying in one accord with one heart, and one mind. By this, they accessed the supply of the Spirit.

> **from whom the whole body, joined and knit together by what every joint *supplies*, according to the effective working by which every part does its share, causes growth of the body for the edifying of itself in love.**
>
> **Ephesians 4:16**

The more that people join together in one accord in one place, the more supply there will be made available to those seeking God. This is not speaking of a distributed supply, because God's supply is unlimited and cannot be exhausted.

> **When the Day of Pentecost had fully come, they were all with one accord in one place.**
>
> **And suddenly there came a sound from heaven, as of a rushing mighty wind, and it filled the whole house where they were sitting.**
>
> **Then there appeared to them divided tongues, as of fire, and one sat upon each of them.**
>
> **And they were all filled with the Holy Spirit** [supply of the Spirit] **and began to speak with other tongues, as the Spirit gave them utterance.**
>
> **Acts 2:1-4**

As is evident in this passage, there is power released during corporate prayer. Another good example of this is found in Second Chronicles chapter five. In this chapter, we see one hundred and twenty priests, along with the Levites, all worshipping God in one accord. As they continue to do this, the glory of God comes down in their midst. When believers join together in one accord to pray, the supply of the Spirit is increased and greater anointings are available for them to draw on. This type of prayer brings an unbelievable increase in the anointing and the ability to access the supply of the Spirit.

So continuing daily with one accord in the temple, and breaking bread from house to house, they ate their food with gladness and simplicity of heart.

...praising God and having favor with all the people. And the Lord added to the church daily those who were being saved.

Acts 2:46,47

And when they had prayed, the place where they were assembled together was shaken; and they were all filled with the Holy Spirit, and they spoke the word of God with boldness.

Acts 4:31

Through the power of corporate prayer, this same group of people received access to the supply of the Spirit and received another infilling of the Holy Spirit. The power of their unified prayers produced great increase.

Filled with God's Supply

It's one thing to possess the Baptizer, but it's another thing to be possessed by the Baptizer. The following message I preach, entitled *Filled with Hagendaas,* is a good example of the difference of being filled with the Holy Spirit and receiving the Holy Spirit.

You can go out and buy some Hagen Daas ice cream, then take it home and put it in the fridge and tell everyone, "I've received Hagen Daas ice cream. Come look in my fridge. Look at the label." It would be accurate to say at this point that you have received Hagendaas ice cream. However, you are not filled with Hagendaas ice cream. You can see what Hagendaas is made of by reading the label. You can know almost everything about Hagendaas ice cream, but until you eat Hagendaas ice cream, you don't know what it tastes like. Until then, you haven't really experienced it. You have to actually open your mouth and swallow, to be filled with Hagendaas ice cream.

You may even go immerse yourself in Hagendaas ice cream. You may look like Hagendaas ice cream is all over you. You may be sticky and sweet with Hagendaas ice cream. But would that mean you were filled with Hagendaas ice cream? You can even share it with others. You can love it and appreciate it, but are you *filled* with Hagendaas?

Every time you're filled with the Holy Spirit, you become more like the Holy Spirit. To put it simply, you are what you eat. If all you eat is Hagendaas ice cream, sooner of later you'll look like Hagendaas ice cream. Every time you are filled with the Holy Ghost you become more like the Holy Ghost. I once heard Rev. David Duplesse, also known as the father of Pentecost, say, "tongues is the consequence of being filled with the Holy Spirit." There is always a consequence of being filled. Every time you're filled with the Holy Ghost, He shows you things to come, and you glorify Jesus. The Father gave me Jesus, and Jesus gave me the Holy Ghost.

In Ephesians, we find an excellent example of being filled with God.

And do not be drunk with wine, in which is dissipation; but be filled with the Spirit.

Ephesians 5:18

...drink deeply of....

(Wey)

...drink deep in the Spirit.

(Mon)

...but be ever filled with the Spirit.

(Wms)

Ephesians 3:19

When we are filled with the Spirit, we're also filled with the fruits of righteousness, wisdom, and understanding.

being filled with the fruits of righteousness which are by Jesus Christ, to the glory and praise of God.

Philippians 1:11

For this reason we also, since the day we heard it, do not cease to pray for you, and to ask that you may be filled with the knowledge of His will in all wisdom and spiritual understanding.

Colossians 1:9

...that you may be filled with all the fullness of God.

(NKJV)

...that you may be filled up to all the fullness of God.

(NASB)

...so at last you will be filled up with God Himself.

(Tay)

Ephesians 3:19

Let's get filled up with God Himself....

---

[1]Lake, p. 27.

48

Chapter 6
Entering In

The Holy of Holies

Entering into God's presence is vital to our understanding, receiving and demonstrating the supply of the Spirit. As children of God, we can enter the Holy of Holies and receive great grace and help in time of need, because the veil has been torn and God has made a way of access for us through the shed blood of His Son, thus enabling us to freely enter into the presence of God.

Then, behold, the veil of the temple was torn in two from top to bottom; and the earth quaked, and the rocks were split.

Matthew 27:51

Therefore, brethren, having boldness to enter the Holiest by the blood of Jesus,

by a new and living way which He consecrated for us, through the veil, that is, His flesh.

Hebrews 10:19,20

Jesus Christ, the Anointed One's anointing has removed the veil. Now we have the fullness of the light of the supply of the Spirit, which overwhelms the light of revelation which comes through the candlesticks in the Holy Place.

49

Just as there were several steps that had to be taken before entering the tabernacle of old, there is, even now, in the New Testament, a divine order — steps that we must take in Christ to access the full riches of His presence and glory.

1. Our hearts must be well pleasing to God.

Enter into His gates with thanksgiving, and into His courts with praise....

Psalm 100:4

The humble shall see this and be glad; and you who seek God, your hearts shall live.

Psalm 69:32

I will praise You, O Lord my God, with all my heart, and I will glorify Your name forevermore.

Psalm 86:12

2. We must be clothed in righteousness.

If we confess our sins, He is faithful and just to forgive us our sins and to cleanse us from all unrighteousness.

1 John 1:9

"Repent therefore and be converted, that your sins may be blotted out, so that times of refreshing may come from the presence of the Lord."

Acts 3:19

"Rain down, you heavens, from above, and let the skies pour down righteousness; let the earth open, let them bring forth salvation, and let righteousness spring up together. I, the LORD, have created it.

Isaiah 45:8

....let the skies rain down righteousness [the pure, spiritual, heaven-born possibilities that have their foundation in the holy being of God]....

Isaiah 45:8 (AMP)

knowing this, that our old man was crucified with Him, that the body of sin might be done away with, that we should no longer be slaves of sin.

Romans 6:6

I beseech you therefore, brethren, by the mercies of God, that you present your bodies a living sacrifice, holy, acceptable to God, which is your reasonable service.

Romans 12:1

that He might sanctify and cleanse her with the washing of the water by the word.

Ephesians 5:26

3. We must be pure in our motives and conduct. Remember that the tabernacle was God's dwelling place. Today, it's a place of spiritual intimacy with God. He desires to be intimate with you so that He can impart the supply of the Spirit to you and enable you to do all that He has called you to do. So as we continue to enter into God's presence, we must wash away all cares, fears, bitterness, unforgiveness, and everything that hinders and weighs us down. Then we can fully know justification and move on in God. We need to learn to let the Word of God purify all of our motives and conduct.

submitting to one another in the fear of God.

Ephesians 5:21

4. Now let's enter into the Holy Place with praise and receive first hand revelation. Move beyond thanking God for the many good things He has done for you, and begin to magnify His character and His loving nature, which are behind all His actions. Praise Him for His love, mercy, grace, long-suffering, and loving-kindness. Praise is beyond thanksgiving. Praise believes on the character of God and His love. Remember that praise

is a *choice* and is not based on your situation or your emotions. Praise is not based on how you feel, but on your decision to "bless the Lord at all times" (Psalm 34:1).

5. Next you come to the Table of Shewbread which was pierced, understanding and discerning the true Bread of Life (Jesus Christ). Submit all your will to God and His plan then go on to receive the overwhelming light of God's glory freely being extended to us because the veil has been removed by Christ. Remember that it's important to eliminate all thoughts that block the beams of God's glory.

casting down arguments and every high thing that exalts itself against the knowledge of God, bringing every thought into captivity to the obedience of Christ.
2 Corinthians 10:5

Renewing your mind to God's Word will bring clarity to you in understanding the supply of the Spirit.

And do not be conformed to this world, but be transformed by the renewing of your mind, that you may prove what is that good and acceptable and perfect will of God.
Romans 12:2

6. Stop listening to what the world says and what your senses say, and start picking up what your spirit says. Pray in the Spirit, *and* remember to interpret what you pray. Expect Him to teach you and instruct you in this process. Then, be determined to obey the instructions the Holy Spirit gives to you.

7. Now step up to the place of intercession and start praising and worshipping God at the golden altar. Don't hold back any expressions of love. The veil is parted and divine right and responsibility is yours. Enter into

the Holy of Holies and worship Him in Spirit and in truth. Yield fully to the Supply of the Spirit.

"But the hour is coming, and now is, when the true worshipers will worship the Father in spirit and truth; for the Father is seeking such to worship Him.

"God is Spirit, and those who worship Him must worship in spirit and truth."

John 4:23,24

God's Presence First

Remember that intimacy is the birthplace for miracles. I will never forget a statement that Benny Hinn made. "So many people want the power of God, but fail to understand that it will not come until they first experience His presence. When the presence comes, the first evidence will be the manifestation of the fruit of the Spirit. The fruit will be evident in every day contact with those around you. When there is genuine fruit, the Lord will anoint you with His Spirit, which is power."

He also said the following in the same message, "The presence of God is the vehicle that brings the power. His presence does not come after His power but rather Power *follows* His presence. The presence and the fruit come together, as do the anointing and the power." God spoke clearly to Benny Hinn, "I don't anoint vessels that are empty of Me. I anoint vessels that are full of Me."

Instead of being self-conscious, with little or no God consciousness, gain God consciousness, and manifest the fruit of God. Fear is the first result of self-consciousness, and boldness is the first result of God consciousness.

The presence of the Spirit will indwell your spirit, while the anointing of the Spirit will cover and saturate you.

It takes the presence of God to change you! And it takes the anointing to communicate that presence out of you.

But the anointing which you have received from Him abides in you, and you do not need that anyone teach you; but as the same anointing teaches you concerning all things, and is true, and is not a lie, and just as it has taught you, you will abide in Him.

1 John 2:27

Chapter 7
Opening Up the Channel

What do I mean by living channels? John G. Lake said, "The Holy Spirit is not simply given that you may be a channel and always a channel. No Sir!! But instead of that, the most magnificent thing the Word of God portrays is that Christ, indwelling in you by the Holy Ghost, is to make you a son of God like Jesus Christ, God anointed from heaven, with recognized power of God in your spirit to command the will of God."[1]

God said in Isaiah 8:18 that He has called His children to signs and wonders. He wants to anoint *us* so that we can cast out devils and heal the sick. He wants *us* to administer the supply of the Spirit so that we literally become a living *channel* of God.

For of Him and through Him and to Him are all things, to whom be glory forever. Amen.

Romans 11:36

"For of him" — this expression doubtless means that he is the original source and fountain of all blessings. He is the Creator of all, the rich fountain from which all streams of existence arise. Note carefully Romans 11:36. It's the last scripture in Romans chapter 11, and is connected with the first scripture in Romans chapter 12. In the original text, they are not separated into chapters. Because of the flow of the supply of the Spirit, it's very important that the living channel is prepared correctly, as in Romans 12:1, to handle all things concerning His supply in Romans 11:36.

> **I appeal to you therefore, brethren, and beg of you in view of [all] the mercies of God, to make a decisive dedication of your bodies [presenting all your members and faculties] as a living sacrifice, holy (devoted, consecrated) and well pleasing to God, which is your reasonable (rational, intelligent) service and spiritual worship.**
>
> **Romans 12:1 (AMP)**

Many of us have allowed the living channels to be clogged with worry, despair, unbelief, strife, and a lack of genuine love and compassion. It's truly the desire of God's heart for us to break through that clogged channel with faith, hope, and love. When we allow these things to operate inside of us on a consistent basis, we open up these living channels for God's abundant supply to come forth.

> **Now on the first day of Unleavened Bread, when they killed the Passover lamb, His disciples said to Him, "Where do You want us to go and prepare, that You may eat the Passover?"**
>
> **And He sent out two of His disciples and said to them, "Go into the city, and a man will meet you carrying a pitcher of water; follow him.**
>
> **"Wherever he goes in, say to the master of the house, 'The Teacher says, "Where is the guest room in which I may eat the Passover with My disciples"'?**
>
> **"Then he will show you a large upper room, furnished and prepared; there make ready for us."**
>
> **Mark 14:12-15**

Now in those days, it was uncommon to see a man carrying a water pitcher, because this was a task only women performed. The disciples probably didn't believe they would find such a man. However, they saw Jesus' many healings and miracles and knew His credibility, so they went ahead and did as He asked them to without question.

A very good application that can be drawn from this story. Some people go about all their lives looking for a man with a water pitcher, someone to pour into their lives. The truth is, instead of spending your life looking for the man with a blessing for you, you should be the man with the water pitcher ready to pour out a blessing on others, first. Jesus became the man with the water pitcher *before* He ever needed the man with the water pitcher. So one of the ways to become a living channel of the supply of the Spirit is to give, and as you give, it will be given unto you. Don't be selfish, but become a water pitcher for someone else to draw from.

Hope

Now may the God of hope fill you with all joy and peace in believing, that you may abound in hope by the power of the Holy Spirit.

Romans 15:13

God desires that we abound in hope. We can accomplish this when we put our hope in Christ. In order for our hope to remain in Him, it has got to be pure and in line with God's will. He has hope in us and in all mankind; so allow Him to "fill you with all joy and peace in believing."

For we were saved in this *hope*, but hope that is seen is not *hope*; for why does one still *hope* for what he sees?

But if we *hope* for what we do not see, we eagerly wait for it with perseverance.

Romans 8:24,25

Although we cannot physically see it, we patiently wait for it to manifest. How? *By the power of the supply of the Spirit.* How do we abound in hope? *By the supply of the Spirit.* By allowing God's Spirit to come and supply us and minister to us. When we touch God, He will touch others through us. The more His Spirit ministers through us, the more we will abound in hope by the power of the Holy Spirit. The Bible states that *Faith is the substance of things hoped for.* Those things, which we are hoping for, will not come through our own works or natural abilities but *only* by the power of the Holy Spirit and the exercise of our *faith*.

The same anointing, the same accesses to the supply that Jesus experienced, He wants us to experience. Hope is an image connecting the natural with the supernatural, using faith as the substance to build a channel into this grace so that we can rejoice in the glory of God. There must be a channel of faith. By hope, faith's channel can raise us into the presence of God to access us to the fullness of God. Hope is that which goes past the veil into the presence of God (Hebrews 6:18,19). Hope is the anchor of the soul, sure and steadfast, immovable. Hope anchors us in the throne room of God. Hope is the earnest expectation of the manifestation of the Word. Because the Anointed One's anointing in us is the hope of glory, the Word becoming flesh, this hope connects us to love.

This is real life.

This is a fountain springing up.

For as the earth brings forth its bud, as the garden causes the things that are sown in it to spring

forth, so the Lord God will cause righteousness and praise to spring forth before all the nations.

Isaiah 61:11

Just like a baby is attached to the mother by the umbilical cord and its nutrients are being supplied by that cord, so, hope anchors us into the presence of God, to the throne room where the rivers are flowing. That supply is coming to us because we are anchored just as a baby is anchored to the mother. Then, out of our bellies will flow forth the rivers of living waters. How does a baby come to the place to where it is self-sustaining to eat from the Father's banqueting table?

"but whoever drinks of the water that I shall give him will never thirst. But the water that I shall give him will become in him a fountain of water springing up into everlasting life."

John 4:14

According to John 4:14, the water God gives us must be similar to a seed with perpetual producing power. The way this is done is through the channel, which takes on the aspects of a fountain of water springing up into everlasting life. We then become more than channels; we become living channels through which the fullness of God can be manifested and displayed.

On the last day, that great day of the feast, Jesus stood and cried out, saying, "If anyone thirsts, let him come to Me and drink.

"He who believes in Me, as the Scripture has said, out of his heart will flow rivers of living water."

But this He spoke concerning the Spirit, whom those believing in Him would receive; for the Holy Spirit was not yet given, because Jesus was not yet glorified.

John 7:37-39

So when Jesus was glorified, the Holy Spirit was poured in order for God to be glorified in us.

And he showed me a pure river of water of life, clear as crystal, proceeding from the throne of God and of the Lamb.

Revelation 22:1

Praise God that we can be anchored in the throne, allowing clear rivers to flow forth out of us!

Faith

Smith Wigglesworth said, "Faith counts on God's coming forth to confound the enemy. Faith counts on the display of God's might when it is needful for Him to come forth in power. We must expect God to come forth in power through us for the deliverance of others. Peter spoke of it as 'like precious faith' (2 Peter 1:1). It is a like kind to that which Abraham had, the very faith of God. When Peter said to the lame man, 'such as I have give I thee: In the name of Jesus Christ of Nazareth rise up and walk' (Acts 3:6), there was manifestation of the same kind of faith that Abraham had. It is this kind of precious faith God wants us to have. Faith in God will bring the operation of the Spirit, and we will have the divine power flooding the human vessel and flowing out in blessing to others. May God help us all to believe, not only for the rivers, but also for the mightiness of His unbounded ocean to flow through us."[2]

Faith is the visionary channel that allows hope (the images and plans of faith) to penetrate beyond the veil. Faith enables us to access the throne of grace to obtain grace and help in the time of need, energized by the love of God, which is shed abroad in our hearts by the Holy Spirit. Faith is the substance of things hoped for, the evidence of things not seen. Faith becomes the substance that accesses us to the throne. There is a room beyond the open veil full of everything we need for the body and soul. Praise, worship, and prayer taps into this supply room and brings it to this side of the open veil into manifestation.

> **Fight the good fight of faith, lay hold on eternal life, to which you were also called and have confessed the good confession in the presence of many witnesses.**
>
> **1 Timothy 6:12**

Faith is the means we use to lay hold on eternal life. As Christians, we are called to "fight the good fight of faith," but what does that actually involve? In the next verse, we see the relationship between faith and hope established.

> **Now faith is the substance of things hoped for, the evidence of things not seen.**
>
> **Hebrews 11:1**

> **...being the proof of things [we] do not see and the conviction of their reality [faith perceiving as real what is not revealed to the senses].**
>
> **Hebrews 11:1 (AMP)**

> **Are you so foolish and so senseless and so silly? Having begun [your new life spiritually] with the [Holy] Spirit, are you now reaching perfection [by dependence] on the flesh?**

> **Have you suffered so many things and experienced so much all for nothing (to no purpose) — if it really is to no purpose and in vain?**

> **Then does He Who *supplies* you with His marvelous [Holy] Spirit and works powerfully and miraculously among you do so [on the grounds of your doing] what the Law demands, or because of**

your believing in and adhering to and trusting in and relying on the message that you heard?

Galatians 3:3-5 (AMP)

He who *supplies* you abundantly with His Spirit and endows you to perform miracles, what is the reason for it? Your observance of the law, or your obedience to the call of faith.

Galatians 3:5 (TCNT)

He therefore that ministereth to you the Spirit, and worketh miracles among you, doeth he it by the works of the law, or by the hearing of faith?

Galatians 3:5 (KJV)

By the hearing of faith.

that Christ may dwell in your hearts *through* faith;...

Ephesians 3:17

How can the Anointed One (Christ means the Anointed One), the very One who said: *"Father the glory that You gave Me I give them that they may be one as we are one"* (John 17:22), come and abide within us?

When Jesus Christ comes in us, He has to come in through faith. Even when we enter the presence of God, we enter it by faith. The Word states: "that Christ may dwell in your hearts through faith." If it's *through* faith, then faith is the *conductor*. Just as electricity is carried through a conductor, the power of God comes to us *through* faith. When we're administering the supply of the Spirit, the Spirit of God and the anointing of God can flow through us *only if* we're operating in faith.

...without faith it is impossible to please Him, [this is because] for he who comes to God must believe that He is, and that He is a rewarder of those who diligently seek Him. **Hebrews 11:6**

Since we can't even enter God's presence without faith, how could we possibly flow in His Spirit without it? When I feel the tangible presence of God on me, and people around me are falling out in the Spirit, the only way His presence can be there is through *faith*. At this point, I don't wonder whether I'm in faith, because love's dominion is flowing, and I know hope is past the veil into the throne where rivers of compassion are flowing. Now I know faith is being energized by love.

When I believe God's word, I have a revelation of His throne room. I am standing before the presence of God and receiving the supply of the Spirit *through faith*. I can't see it with my physical eyes, but by faith I enter into the throne room of God and receive the supply of the Spirit, so that I can administer it to others. As I enter His presence in faith, the revelation becomes more complete in me.

So then faith comes by hearing, and hearing by the word of God.
Romans 10:17

...We conclude that faith is awakened by the message....
Romans 10:17 (NEB)

To see a free flow of the supply of the Spirit, faith must be awakened. Faith comes by hearing and hearing by the Word of God. The more we hear His Word, the more our conductor is established and the more we are able to administer the supply of the spirit. Remember when Jesus operated in the anointing and administered the supply of the Spirit, removing burdens and destroying yokes? Jesus was moved by compassion. I like to call compassion love's dominion, because love is the more excellent way. First Corinthians 13:13 says, "concerning faith, hope, and love; love is the greatest." Scripture never indicates that Jesus did anything by faith as God's men and women did in Hebrews 11. Scripture says that Jesus is the Author and Finisher of our faith. Faith is energized and finds its full expression in love.

For [if we are] in Christ Jesus, neither circumcision nor uncircumcision counts for anything, but only faith activated and energized and expressed and working through love.

Galatians 5:6 (AMP)

Once we are in Christ, circumcision means nothing, and the want of it means nothing; the faith that finds its expression in love is all that matters.

Galatians 5:6 (Knox)

Faith works by love because love is the *energy* or battery that drives God's life through the conductor of faith. Love draws the supply of the Spirit right through the visionary channel of faith into us.

Believe that God's love has been shed abroad in your heart by the Holy Spirit and is continually working in you, spirit, soul, and body.

God is love. That's why the Word says:

that Christ may dwell in your hearts through faith; that you, being rooted and grounded in love,

Ephesians 3:17

We certainly do not want a run down or weak battery. That is precisely why we must be rooted and grounded in love. In the same way a tree receives the supply of nutrients from its roots, we are supplied by the power of love. If a tree can draw good nutrients through the roots, then it will be strong and healthy, yielding healthy fruits.

Our love has got to be strong! The more we reach out in love, the greater our capacity will be to administer the supply of the Spirit; as our heavenly Father's love grows in us, so will the supply of the Spirit increase.

> **but, speaking the truth in love, may grow up in all things into Him who is the head — Christ —**
>
> **from whom the whole body, joined and knit together by what every joint supplies, according to the effective working by which every part does its share, causes growth of the body for the edifying of itself in love.**
>
> **Ephesians 4:15,16**

The increase of the supply of the Spirit brings edification to the body of Christ. The increase of the supply enables us to reach out in love in a greater capacity, enabling us to edify and build each other up. The stronger our love is, the easier it will be to administer the supply of the Spirit. This is due to the fact that miracles will go as far as our love goes. Those of us who are weak in the area of love can develop a stronger love. This happens when we recognize that our Spirit man (or hidden man of the heart) can receive an *unlimited* supply of love from God's Spirit. The increase of the supply of the Spirit is according to the effectual working of the saints in prayer, interceding out of love, not just need. Aren't you glad that Jesus is making intercession for us, not because we need it, but because of compassion?

Every member of the body of Christ must work together. It takes all the members of the body of Christ to make up the different types of the anointing. There are also different gifts in the body of Christ, all working together through different members of the body. This will only be accomplished through love. Through accessing the supply of the Spirit, the different anointings are able to increase within the body of Christ. This love only works through faith, faith brings the supply of the Spirit and provides us with access into the kingdom of God. Not only does love enable our faith to work, but the guaranteed supply of it, energizes our hope as well.

Now hope does not disappoint, because the love of God has been poured out in our hearts by the Holy Spirit who was given to us.
Romans 5:5

We can see that the love of God (Agape, the God kind of love), or as the original translation states, God's capacity to love, has been shed abroad in our hearts by the Holy Ghost. *We have the potential to love just as much as God loves*! As we exercise the love *poured out* by the Spirit we will bear the image of the heavenly Man by the Spirit of God. When we allow ourselves to be moved by the very love and compassion of God, our new nature will experience a greater intimacy and fellowship with the Father.

O God, You are my God; early will I seek You, my soul thirsts for You; my flesh longs for You in a dry and thirsty land where there is no water.
Psalm 63:1

"Oh God, I've got to come and drink from You, for your love is better than wine. I want intimacy with you Father." This is the cry of the love nature. God says: "come up to the mountain with Me, My love, My bride." He's calling us. He wants intimacy with us. When we begin to pour out our love to God, and we see someone sick, the very love and compassion of God will rise up inside. It begins to draw from the resources that are energizing our faith. Faith and love begin to work together. Then, the resources of God begin to flow, the supply of the Spirit begins to flow, and we then administer the supply of the Spirit to others."

---

1 Lake, p. 152

2 Warner, p. 91

Chapter 8
Administering the Supply

But Jesus said, Someone did touch Me; for I perceived that [healing] power has gone forth from Me.

Luke 8:46 (AMP)

Divine Flow

In this scripture, Jesus felt the supply of the Spirit go out of Him. This clearly shows a divine flow of God's power, and when we walk in *faith* and *hope* propelled by a pure *love* motive, we can perceive when it's coming and going. This perception grows, as we become more in tune with the Anointed One's anointing. Notice the benefits:

Therefore, if anyone is in Christ, he is a new creation; old things have passed away; behold, all things have become new.

2 Corinthians 5:17

As the supply of the Spirit begins to flow, we can truly sense how God has made us a new creation. When the verse states, "if anyone is in Christ," it says literally, if anyone is in the Anointed One. As a new creation we are born anew to administer that supply. As we yield to the supply of the Spirit, it ministers to us; we gain access to the supply and administer this supply to others. It is a gift meant to be given out, *"Freely you have received, freely give."* Do not hold the anointing back!

The more we release the supply of the Spirit and the anointing, the more it will grow. Our miracle is living inside of us (Christ in you the Hope of glory). Jesus the Healer and His very nature are alive inside of us. As we yield to that nature and allow the supply of the Spirit to flow out of us, sickness will not be able to withstand it. Second Peter states that we are made partakers of His nature. At this point, it's inevitable that *we will have healings and miracles.*

by which have been given to us exceedingly great and precious promises, that through these you may be partakers of the divine nature, having escaped the corruption that is in the world through lust.

2 Peter 1:4

By means of these He has bestowed on us His precious and exceedingly great promises, so that through them you may escape [by flight] from the moral decay (rottenness and corruption) that is in the world because of covetousness (lust and greed), and become sharers (partakers) of the divine nature.

2 Peter 1:4 (AMP)

Those who receive the promises of the Gospel, partake of the divine nature. They are renewed in the spirit of their mind, after the image of God, in knowledge, righteousness, and holiness; their hearts are set for God and his service. That *is* the supply of the Spirit. When we allow the presence of God within us to flow through us and into others, we cause them to be changed and healed by the power of God, because of the supply that we administer to them. The supply of the Spirit within us will burn out sin and sickness, because impurities cannot abide within the same channel. Remember, it is *Christ in you that is the Hope of Glory.* We have a right to hope (in faith and love) that His glory will be demonstrated through us.

The Word of God says that we will know a tree by its fruit and that God's desire for us is that we bear much fruit. In order for that fruit to be evident in our lives, we must be drawing from His supply and administering it to others. The more we administer that supply to others, the greater God's power will be manifested through us.

John G. Lake said, "I call you today, beloved, by the grace of God, to that high life, to that holy walk, to that heavenly atmosphere, to that life in God where the grace and Spirit and power of God permeates our whole being. More, where not only your whole being is in subjection, but it flows from your nature as a holy stream of heavenly life to bless other souls everywhere by the grace of God."[1]

But to each one is given the manifestation of the [Holy] Spirit [the evidence, the spiritual illumination of the Spirit] for good and profit.

1 Corinthians 12:7 (AMP)

Once again we see how God is establishing a living channel for a fountain of living water to rise from your nature.

Overcomers

As God's power begins to flow through us, we'll walk as overcomers. When we begin to walk in the anointing of God (and drink from the Rock that is Christ), the Anointed One's anointing will remove burdens and destroy yokes.

In Ezekiel, we see how God prepares hearts for increase so there can be no lack of the supply.

"Then I will sprinkle clean water on you, and you shall be clean; I will cleanse you from all your filthiness and from all your idols.

"I will give you a new heart and put a new spirit within you; I will take the heart of stone out of your flesh and give you a heart of flesh.

"I will deliver you from all your uncleanness. I will call for the grain and multiply it, and bring no famine upon you.

"And I will multiply the fruit of your trees and the increase of your fields, so that you need never again bear the reproach of famine among the nations."

Ezekiel 36:25,26,29,30

Abiding in the presence of the Anointed One's anointing will kill sin, if we allow the anointing oil of the supply of the Spirit to flow through us. When we walk in the Spirit, we will not fulfill the lust of the flesh:

It shall come to pass in that day that his burden will be taken away from your shoulder, and his yoke from your neck, and the yoke will be destroyed because of the anointing oil.

Isaiah 10:27

Great Grace

Grace in *Strong's Concordance*, is defined as "the divine influence upon the heart and its reflection in the life."[2] This is speaking of great increase both physically and spiritually. In Acts 4:33,34 and Acts 5:15, there was none of the church of that time that lacked for anything, and, as Peter casts shadows, all the sick were healed. There was a great supply of increase coming from the throne upon the heart and being reflected in the life in a radiance of anointing producing glory in those oppressed by the devil, driving out all sickness and bringing to the people total healing, health, and wholeness in all areas.

To minister and release the supply of the Spirit, is to bring healing; it is to permit the divine influence upon the heart and its reflection in the life to flow through you physically to others. In this we can see grace having free rule and reign in one's life.

The supply of the Spirit will also bring rain.

The Lord will answer and say to His people, "Behold, I will send you grain and new wine and oil, and you will be satisfied by them; I will no longer make you a reproach among the nations."

Be glad then, you children of Zion, and rejoice in the Lord your God; for He has given you the former rain faithfully, and He will cause the rain to come down for you — the former rain, and the latter rain in the first month.

The threshing floors shall be full of wheat, and the vats shall overflow with new wine and oil.

Joel 2:19,23,24

It takes rain for us to be full of wheat and for the vats to have new wine and oil. To have the things that God desires for us, it will take drinking of the living water. The rain brings corn which strengthens and nourishes. This is the bread of life.

"I also withheld rain from you, when there were still three months to the harvest. I made it rain on one city, I withheld rain from another city. One part was rained upon, and where it did not rain the part withered.

"So two or three cities wandered to another city to drink water, but they were not satisfied; yet you have not returned to Me," says the Lord.

Amos 4:7,8

We can run to every revival we want, but until we seek God and come and drink of His presence, we will not be satisfied. It takes something to get the Holy Ghost water and rain; it involves separateness, and singleness of vision. The rivers of God must be flowing through us. We must be soul-winning stations.

The peace of God is directly related to our prayer life. Our victory is a direct reflection of our prayer life. Some people wonder why they don't have victory. When it *rains*, we'll *have* wheat, new wine, and oil this is a direct reflection of our prayer lives.

We must pray. This will keep us from becoming stubborn. It will also enable us to receive wheat so we'll have bread and oil to give to others so we can celebrate the freedom that is in Christ. If we give to others, the rain will continually fall on us, so that we can keep on giving.

Ask the Lord for rain in the time of the latter rain. The Lord will make flashing clouds; He will give them showers of rain, grass in the field for everyone.

Zechariah 10:1

Flowing Out

A lot of people talk about the anointing to remove burdens and destroy yokes. Although this is an important aspect of the anointing, there's also another aspect of the anointing. It has to do with pouring in the oil and the wine (like the parable of the good Samaritan). What does pouring in the oil and the wine represent? It represents healing and restoration. When the anointing flows through us, it administers healing and restoration to those who need it.

The wine is the joy of the Lord. Isaiah 55 says to come and buy priceless spiritual wine without price, simply for self surrender. There are people sitting and waiting for the river of life to come to them, but Jesus is standing before us saying, "I am the healer. I am the river of life. I am the waters that flow out to you with healing. I am the water that flows with joy. I am the waters that flow with peace." Jesus is the river of life. The river of life gives rest, refreshing, and peace.

When Jesus turned the water into wine, He said that He did it to show forth His *glory*. This reminds me of a time when we were at a friend's house and a little boy came from across the street with his mother. The boy was sick because of an infection in his ears, causing him pain and discomfort. His mother wanted to see if we could give them some medicine for his pain. We told them to come in and we would pray for them. Now understand, that the little boy and his mother had no faith in the power of God. In fact, they were not even Christians. Nevertheless, I felt the anointing on me, laid hands on him and commanded his ears to be healed. Suddenly, the little boy turned around and looked at his mother and said: "The pain is gone, I don't feel anymore pain." For about the next twenty minutes or so, the mother kept asking him how he felt. He just kept telling her that he didn't feel any more pain. This has been God's plan all along, to have the oil and wine of healing and comfort *flowing out* to the world through us, His body.

Anointed

In the Gospel of Matthew, Peter is recorded as saying to Jesus: "You are the Christ, the Son of the Living God." In response, Jesus turned around and said: "Peter, flesh and blood has not revealed this to you, but My

Father which is in heaven." Later on, however, He commands the disciples not to tell anyone that He's the Christ. By saying this, He was essentially saying: "Do not tell anyone that I am the Messiah, anointed with God's power to heal the sick and cast out devils." It was not yet time for them to proclaim this because they had not yet received His anointing.

The disciples were not anointed until God poured out His Holy Spirit on them in the upper room. Then, they immediately began to proclaim and to preach the good news of the Gospel of *Christ*, the Anointed One and His anointing. They began to proclaim the Anointed One and His anointing and how this anointing was now available for them. They began to administer the supply of the Spirit. Before this, they had no authority to administer the supply of the Spirit, because they had not yet received the supply of the Spirit themselves.

In the same way, we have no authority to administer the supply of the Spirit, *until* we receive that same supply. A Christian who has not yet been endued with the power of the Holy Spirit can preach the Lord Jesus as Savior, but how can they possibly get someone else filled with the supply of the Spirit, when they are not filled themselves? We cannot administer something that we do not have. It stands to reason, that unless we come into the experience of Christ's anointing, we have no authority to administer it to others. Those of us in the world who would receive the Spirit, will be drawn in by the "magnetic" aspect of the anointing that abides within us. When we enter into the presence of God by His word and access the supply of the Spirit, we then have the authority to administer the supply of the Spirit to others.

Colossians says that in *Christ* are hidden *all* the treasures of wisdom and knowledge. That is literally stating that in *God's Anointed One* and *His anointing,* all wisdom and knowledge can be found. The Bible says we can ask God for wisdom and knowledge, and He will give it to us (providing we ask *in faith:* James 1:5,6). This is crucial because we need an *anointed mind.* When we have an anointed mind, we enable the supply of the Spirit to flow through us; thus we can administer the supply of the Spirit under the unction of the Holy Spirit.

---

[1]Lake, p. 50.

[2]James Strong, *Strong's Exhaustive Concordance of the Bible* (Tennessee: Manna Publishers), p. 77.

Chapter 9

Hindrances to the
Flow of the Supply

There are several things that inhibit the flow of the supply of the Spirit within us that we need to be aware of and guard against. Hebrew 12:28 says that "we may serve God acceptably with reverence and godly fear." It is important for us to realize that unless we are serving God in the power of the supply of the Spirit, we are not able to administer the supply of the Spirit to those around us; thus, we become an ineffective tool for the kingdom of God.

1. Having wrong motives will hinder the flow of the supply of the Spirit. What is our motive for serving God? The Bible says that we need to judge ourselves. We need to judge our motives.

2. Strife will hinder or block the flow of the supply of the Spirit. We must live Holy and be peacemakers.

Nevertheless the solid foundation of God stands, having this seal: "The Lord knows those who are His," and, "Let everyone who names the name of Christ depart from iniquity."

But in a great house there are not only vessels of gold and silver, but also of wood and clay, some for honor and some for dishonor.

Therefore if anyone cleanses himself from the latter, he will be a vessel for honor, sanctified and useful for the Master, prepared for every good work.

Flee also youthful lusts; but pursue righteousness, faith, love, peace with those who call on the Lord out of a pure heart.

But avoid foolish and ignorant disputes, knowing that they generate strife.

2 Timothy 2:19-23

The body of Christ must walk in purity and unity avoiding any kind of strife.

3. Neglecting to spend time with God in His Word and in prayer will hinder the flow of the supply of the Spirit.

But He answered and said, "It is written, 'Man shall not live by bread alone, but by every word that proceeds from the mouth of God.'"

Matthew 4:4

Be diligent to present yourself approved to God, a worker who does not need to be ashamed, rightly dividing the word of truth.

2 Timothy 2:15

4. Engaging in worthless and unwholesome speech will hinder the supply of the Spirit. If what you are about to say doesn't edify or move someone closer to the kingdom of God, don't say it.

Let no corrupt word proceed out of your mouth, but what is good for necessary edification, that it may impart grace to the hearers.

Ephesians 4:29

5. *Use* the gifts God has given you, or the river will dry up.

> **Therefore I remind you to stir up the gift of God which is in you through the laying on of my hands.**
>
> **2 Timothy 1:6**

6. Letting the "cares of this world" weigh you down; failing to roll your cares over on Him who cares for you will hinder the flow of the supply of the Spirit!

> **"And these are the ones by the wayside where the word is sown. When they hear, Satan comes immediately and takes away the word that was sown in their hearts.**
>
> **"These likewise are the ones sown on stony ground who, when they hear the word, immediately receive it with gladness;**
>
> **"and they have no root in themselves, and so endure only for a time. Afterward, when tribulation or persecution arises for the word's sake, immediately they stumble.**
>
> **"Now these are the ones sown among thorns; they are the ones who hear the word,**
>
> **"and the cares of this world, the deceitfulness of riches, and the desires for others things entering in choke the word, and it becomes unfruitful.**
>
> **"But these are the ones sown on good ground, those who hear the word, accept it, and bear fruit: some thirtyfold, some sixty, and some a hundred."**
>
> **Mark 4:15-20**

Be on constant guard!

7. Not respecting the ministry gifts God has placed in the church will keep the supply of the Spirit from being able to flow freely into you.

And He gave Himself some to be apostles, some prophets, some evangelists, and some pastors and teachers.

Ephesians 4:11

Now you are the body of Christ, and members individually.

And God has appointed these in the church: first apostles, second prophets, third teachers, after that miracles, then gifts of healings, helps, administrations, varieties of tongues.

1 Corinthians 12:27,28

8. The fear of man shuts down the flow of the supply. I have seen the Word compromised and the Holy Spirit reserved for Sunday nights or Wednesday nights only in order not to offend those who might not "understand." God refuses to be placed in a box. Many people get offended and begin recalling human imperfections. When we take offense at the vessel God has sent, we look at the man, in place of the glory that God is releasing through that servant. By doing this we exercise unbelief, and by doing so, stop the supply of the Spirit in our midst.

I charge you therefore before God and the Lord Jesus Christ, who will judge the living and the dead at His appearing and His kingdom:

Preach the Word! Be ready in season and out of season. Convince, rebuke, exhort, with all long-suffering and teaching.

For the time will come when they will not endure sound doctrine, but according to their own desires, because they have itching ears, they will heap up for themselves teachers;

and they will turn their ears away from the truth, and be turned aside to fables.

2 Timothy 4:1-4

9. Not being *faithful* to our call or ministry will shut down the flow of the supply of the Spirit. How hungry are you for God? How thirsty are you for God? How desperate are you for the move of the Holy Spirit?

Blessed are those who hunger and thirst for righteousness, for they shall be filled.

Matthew 5:6

10. Disobedience to the prompting of the Holy Spirit will hinder the flow. When you realize you missed it, repent and get back on track as soon as you possibly can. Do not let your head get in the way! I've heard it said, "Don't touch it (the prompting and direction of the Spirit) with your head!" Although God does want you to use your renewed mind, the anointing originates from your spirit, not your head!

Closing Thoughts

The more we *obey* the Holy Spirit, the more the power of God is released through us. As the flow of the gifts of the Spirit and the anointing of God increase, the supply of the Spirit is going to flow out and minister to others. When we are led to minister to someone by the power of the Holy Spirit, no matter where we are, we need to *obey* immediately. As we do, there will be the supply of the Spirit that we need for that moment.

Jesus said, go into the highways and byways, and the disciples replied, "what are we going to say when we get there?" Jesus told them not to worry about what they were going to speak; just open your mouth, and He will fill it. Jesus stated, "I will give you the words to say at that time." We might not know what we're going to say, but by our obedience, we are accessing the very supply of His Spirit. Obedience allows the supply of the Holy Spirit to come to us and flow out through us.

The power of God is released to the degree that obedience is exercised. By obeying God, we're presenting a yielded will. A yielded will is also an anointed will. I believe an anointed will is the mind of Christ. It's a will that is allowing the supply of the Spirit to flow through it.

Closing Thoughts...A Servant's Heart

Andrew Murray said, "He simply taught us the blessed truth that there is nothing so divine and heavenly as being the servant and helper of all. The faithful servant who recognizes his position finds a real pleasure in supplying the wants of the master or his guests."[1]

This is in keeping with my own eager desire and persistent expectation and hope, that I shall not disgrace myself nor be put to shame in anything; but that with the utmost freedom of speech and unfailing courage, now as always heretofore, Christ (the Messiah) [the Anointed One] will be magnified and get glory and praise in this body of mine and be boldly exalted in my person, whether through (by) life or through (by) death.

Philippians 1:20 (AMP)

Paul proclaims *"to live is Christ."* The main reason that Paul stayed alive was to administer Christ and allow the supply of the Spirit to minister through him. *"That Christ may be magnified in my body:"* In this passage, the word body means Paul's *physical* body. Another translation says: "Your whole being, spirit, soul, and body." If Christ is *magnified* in our whole being, then sickness and disease cannot conquer us.

The glory of God is flowing from the most Holy Place into the "inner court" and the "outer court," manifesting itself in our flesh. As we lay anointed hands on people, the very power of God *will* flow through us.

There are such things as anointed words. The love and compassion of God stirs up the anointing. The anointing flows through the words, but it also flows through us in a physical aspect. In the Old Testament, the prophet Elijah laid upon the body of the dead boy, and he came back to life. He released the power of God into him *physically*.

There is no limit to God's flow, and God's love. That is what God wants to do for us. He wants us to be active and alive with the anointing springing from our very nature.

Smith Wigglesworth wrote, "When our whole lives are surged by the power of God, we become subjects of the Spirit of the living God and we are moved by the almightiness of God. Then we live and move and have our being in this flow of God's wonder-working power. "God is able to make all grace abound" (2 Corinthians 9:8). We are no longer the same person. We have received the mighty anointing power of God, and in this place we realize that the only thing for us to do is to submit to God, and, as we submit, we are more and more covered with power and led by the Spirit."[2]

---

[1]Andrew Murray, *Humility* (Pennsylvania: Whitaker House, 1982), p.7.
[2]Warner, pp.218, 145.

The Vision of Sword Ministries

The foundation of this ministry rests in Hebrews 4:12 which is summarized in the following statement, "Speaking the Truth in Revival, Piercing the Innermost Being." We are to remain carriers of revival, "Demonstrating Signs and Wonders, Decently and In Order, by the Power of the Holy Spirit."

Our vision is to see the stadiums of America and around the world filled to capacity in which the fullness of the Gospel of Christ, the Anointed One is declared unto salvation. Not just in persuasive words of man's wisdom, but in demonstration of the Spirit and in Power (Acts 2), which includes salvation according to Acts 10:44.

To see multitudes touched by the loving presentation of the power of God through power packed spirit filled books published in many different languages, world wide multi-media television and radio productions, and churches and Bible schools established in China and other nations, via Apostolic teams and multi-faceted Evangelistic operations.